T0045010

SCHIRMER'S LIBRARY
OF MUSICAL CLASSICS

Vol. 2045

WOLFGANG AMADEUS MOZART

Piano Concerto No. 26, K. 537

"Coronation Concerto"

For Piano and Orchestra

Edited and Reconstructed by Paul Badura-Skoda

ISBN 978-0-634-01085-9

G. SCHIRMER, Inc.

DISTRIBUTED BY

HAL•LEONARD®
CORPORATION

7777 W. BLUEMOUND RD. P.O. BOX 13819 MILWAUKEE, WI 53213

Preface to the New Revision and Completion of
Mozart's Coronation Concerto, KV 537

The case of the Piano Concerto in D Major, KV 537, is unique in the history of music: In this work Mozart notated the orchestral score and the upper system of the solo part with great care; however, he left large sections of the lower system of the piano part, decidedly for the accompaniment, blank. Only in those few passages where the left hand plays virtuosic runs or has its own motives or opposing contrapuntal lines was it carefully notated.

A lack of time is in all probability the cause for this incomplete notation. Had this work been published during his lifetime, Mozart would most certainly have filled in the remaining passages. One has instead the impression that Mozart had somehow already thought of his afterlife: To fill in purely accompanying figures with the correct harmony apparently appeared to him as a relatively simple task, one that a later musician skilled in Mozart's style could execute without further ado. Indeed, a completion of the present work was rather quickly attempted. In 1794, three years after Mozart's death, this concerto was printed by the composer's admirer Johann André for his own publishing house and with a complete accompaniment. The title page of this edition states that Mozart performed this concerto together with the F Major Concerto, KV 459, for the coronation of Emperor Leopold II in Frankfurt on the 15th of October, 1790—hence earning the name as we know it today: "Coronation Concerto." (In any case, this was not the world premiere—Mozart had already performed the work in Dresden in April of 1789, as he reported in a letter to his wife.) André makes no mention of the many missing notes in the autograph that were completed in his edition, obviously by himself; André was a competent *singspiel* composer who also completed a number of Mozart's other unfinished works. By and large André's effort deserves praise. As the original manuscript was for a long time inaccessible, it is understandable that the music world should have believed the accompaniment to be authentic. Therefore this version continued to be printed by all publishers up until the very present. It was not until the *Neue Mozart Ausgabe* that its editor, Dr. Wolfgang Rehm, came upon the praiseworthy idea of reproducing those parts that are not originally from Mozart in smaller print. In addition, he corrected a few of André's most blatant errors, which merit discussion here: With all due respect to André's effort, he committed a number of rather blunt voice-leading errors. To mention but two of the most important: In measures 45-46 and 50-51 of the second movement he wrote parallel fifths, and in the final measure he wrote a bass part (the first beat of the piano part, l.h.) that does not even match the harmony! Also in the outer movements he managed frequently to write wrong harmonies and awkward accompaniments. However, André's primary fault, from today's standpoint, was his capacity to be too "verbose" in comparison to Mozart's model; where Mozart in all probability wanted rests, André would insert stereotypical accompanying figures. In contrast to André, we have today a knowledge of Mozart's complete works, which gives us more possibilities for attempting a more stylistically exact reconstruction by referring to analogous passages in other works. The study of Mozart's accompanying figures in his piano concertos and sonatas reveals nothing less than an inexhaustible and multifaceted capacity for invention. For the concertos one easily discovers the following principle: When the piano quotes a theme that also comes in the orchestral tutti, the accompaniment nearly always follows the example of the tutti. At the same time, it is simplified enough to be easily playable. From this vantage point it can be seen that André is guilty of quite a few inaccuracies, especially in the graceful second theme of the first movement, where he deviates strongly from the original. Also, the fact that he introduces the accompanying figure one measure before the entry of this theme is un-Mozartian. On the other hand, André's accompaniment of the beginning of the second movement is markedly skillful and agreeable, with the exception of a rather clumsy voice-leading in the third and fourth measures, where he deviates from the ensuing tutti. The beginning of the piano solo in the first movement is well executed. Here André took on the accompanying figure that Mozart, as an exception, wrote out at the beginning of the third movement. (The identical accompaniment also appears in the quite similarly shaped first solo of the E-flat Concerto, K. 482.) In such cases there is no doubt as to whether or not to retain André's version.

What could be done for those solo passages where there were no analogous examples evident in the orchestra? Here there was only one method: to find similarly constructed passages in other works of Mozart and come to a corresponding conclusion. Astonishing parallels exist in the immediately preceding and following piano concertos, K. 503 (1786) and K. 595 (1790-91). By choosing such similarities in parallel passages within this concerto and in other works of Mozart as my starting point, I have attempted to come as close as possible to Mozart's intentions. I have naturally retained André's additions in those passages where they could be considered musically and stylistically successful.

First Movement

As mentioned, André's accompaniment of the first solo (m. 81 ff.) is optimal and was retained. But already seven measures later (m. 87), André deviates from the original harmony of the tutti and adds a pleasant, albeit primitive accompaniment (see footnote in score). His Alberti bass in m. 89 and the parallel passage in m. 300 hardly correspond to Mozart's intentions; Mozart himself preferred long, stationary harmonies in similar passages in the opening solos of the concertos, K. 482 (m. 89 ff.) and K. 503 (m. 103). In m. 90, André brings an independent contrary motion to the strings, which is cute in itself but which appears only seldomly in Mozart's original works. André's first grave error is the unnecessary chord in m. 96. In similar passages of other works Mozart writes rests, for example in K. 503, m. 109.

Also, André's accompaniment in mm. 127-135 is problematic. Due to the busy eighth-note accompaniment on one hand, and to the unnecessary octave doubling (mm. 130-131 and 134-135) on the other, the poetic meaning of this passage is coarsened. The melodic voice-leading of the bass in m. 132 comes across as "plugged up."

Example 1: K. 537/i, mm. 127-135, André's version:

It is a matter of chance that Mozart composed a similarly demonstrative foray into the minor key, in a functionally identical passage in his Piano Concerto, K. 595, whose accompaniment naturally served as my model. In spite of the difference in direction, the relation of the two passages is unmistakable:

Example 2: K. 595/i, mm. 106-112:

Example 3: K. 537/i, Reconstruction of mm. 127-133 by Paul Badura-Skoda:

Measures 145-160 were written out by Mozart himself. The addition of the G-sharp in the bass (m. 152) is thus unnecessary. The conformity to m. 136, where the same figure is repeated a fourth higher, has therefore not been added, since the bass G-sharp in m. 152 thickens the sound. In m. 163, André wrote an accompaniment to the trill that is acceptable in and of itself, as it appears for instance at the end of the D Major Rondo, K. 485, or the third movement of the Sonata in B-flat, K. 570. In contrast, this accompaniment figure rarely appears in Mozart's piano concertos. Further, in this passage it leads to a doubling of the thirds in the first violin and anticipates—as mentioned above—the accompaniment of the following theme (m. 164 ff.).

As already mentioned, André committed a number of errors in working out the secondary theme. In the second half of m. 164 the F-sharp is missing in the accompaniment, in the same section he adds an unjustified dominant seventh, and in m. 167 one would expect the ever so Mozartian tenths and sixths, which I took from other works. Here it was not at all easy to find a version that harmonically approached the tutti original (mm. 38-42) and nonetheless still sounded graceful. The model for a melodically self-contained counter-voice in the left hand was in this case not only the mentioned tutti version, but also the secondary theme of the D Major Sonata, K. 311. (It is no accident that the emotional characters of the individual keys played a significant role for Mozart, such that a number of his works in D major are related to one another.)

The accompaniment starting from the beginning of the development yielded itself almost effortlessly. Only in m. 239 does the B in André's accompaniment appear inappropriate, since it produces a discord with the B-flat, the first note in the right hand. The exceptionally simple accompaniment at the beginning of the development of the opening movement of the C Major Concerto, K. 467, served as a model. André's accompaniment figures are also adequate from m. 263 onwards; I have added only the A in the left hand in mm. 268-269. By and large the previous comments are valid for the recapitulation starting in m. 300. Only in the new motive in m. 388, which is missing in the piano exposition, does it certainly not conform to Mozart's intentions to compose a second accompaniment part in eighths in addition to the eighth notes of the orchestra. My model for this section was a similar motive in the Piano Concerto in E-flat, K. 271 (m. 271 ff.), as well as the piano's very similar answer to the strings in the first movement of the G Major Concerto, K. 453 (mm. 147 and 149). In m. 344, André unnecessarily changed the whole note of the exposition (m. 160) to a quarter note. In mm. 401-403 it was likely more in keeping with Mozart's intentions to support the ascending right hand with an ascent in the accompaniment harmonies. A good alternative, however, is to double and thus reinforce the wind instruments.

v

Second Movement: Larghetto

For the accompaniment in the theme of the second movement, the written out tutti (mm. 9-17) was, of course, the standard to which I leaned toward more closely than André. This movement also displays similarities in structure to the Romance of the D minor Concerto.[1] In that movement there are always notes connecting solo with tutti (or likewise tutti with solo) at the junctures. In mm. 16-17 of the Coronation Concerto Mozart composed a rhythmically similar transition from the tutti to the solo part. Most likely he intended an identical connection from the closing of the solo part to the entrance of the tutti in m. 9 as well as later in m. 79. Since he did not notate this for the melody, it appeared obvious to me to transfer the inferred notes of m. 16 to the left hand. (An alternative version is taken literally from the D minor Concerto.)

More difficult was the reconstruction of mm. 17-27, since there is no model in the tutti for this motive. However, the continuation of the rondo theme (mm. 17 ff.) in the third movement of the E-flat Concerto, K. 482, is very similar. The accompanying figure, taken from that passage, also works quite naturally in the Coronation Concerto. Of course, a new way had to be found starting in m. 19 since Mozart deviates there from K. 482. The "sweet" Mozartian tenths suggested themselves effortlessly and have a more poetic effect than André's Alberti figures.

I do not believe that the theme of this movement should be varied upon its return. In his late works Mozart often preferred unornamented ritornellos in his middle movements, as in the C major Piano Sonata, K. 521, for four hands, which during his lifetime was printed without any ornamentation in the da capo of the Andante. Also in the symphonies composed during the same year, especially that in E-flat, K. 543, the Andante theme is never varied.[2] This is different in the piano's long cantilena in the middle section starting in m. 44: It works just as stated, all too sparsely, especially mm. 49-51. Excited by Mozart's comment in one of his letters, regarding a passage in the second movement of the D major Concerto, K. 451, I allowed myself to propose several discrete ornaments and of course also to ornament the fermata in mm. 70-71. In m. 105 Mozart, as an exception, did not notate the right hand part. (He also did not write rests!) The parallels to the preceding m. 103 are plain, however; therefore, I completed this passage with a similar run.

Third Movement: Allegretto

In the third movement there were relatively few problems, not least of all because Mozart notated the accompaniment himself in numerous passages or at least suggested it. It is not simply a matter of luck that already at the beginning the left-hand figures are written out. They could be—as previously mentioned—used for the first piano solo in the first movement, which André already recognized. These figures are also suitable for the second solo (from m. 48). For mm. 54-55 and the parallel passage (mm. 194-195), the identical usage (mm. 159-160) in the first movement of the A major Piano Concerto, K. 414, served as the model. André inserted the note A in m. 55, which is not technically an error but which expands the previous three voices to four. On the other hand, his accompanying harmonies in the following passages were carried out rather clumsily. In mm. 126-129 the piano followed the winds (quarter notes), while Mozart in such places in other concertos fit the piano part to the strings (e.g. K. 467, third movement, m. 128 ff.). The accompaniment notated by Mozart in m. 136 allows for the conclusion that he did not intend the same figure to be used for the preceding measure, as is printed in André's edition.

Small problems arise at the end of the movement, in the coda. The figure in the right hand in m. 344 is identical to a passage in the Concert Rondo, K. 386 (m. 217 ff.). Clearly the accompaniment should be carried out in three voices as in K. 386. André's execution of mm. 352-354 (and why not also mm. 346-348?) can be considered agreeable. On the other hand, his figurations in the last two measures of the solo part (mm. 368-396) called for improvement.

[1] In the only extant sketch for the Coronation Concerto, Mozart also wrote "Romance" as the title of the second movement.
[2] In several of the piano sonatas printed during the composer's lifetime, Mozart added ornamented variants that are not found in the autographs. The slow movements of the piano sonatas in F major, K. 332, and C minor, K. 457, offer typical examples. Obviously he did not trust his interpreters to invent good ornaments. The case of Hoffmann, who shortly after Mozart's death composed terrible ornaments, shows just how correct Mozart was. Conversely, if he did not print any variants, it means most likely that he desired a literal repeat in the da capo.

It has been repeatedly remarked that the winds in this concerto play a subordinate roll in comparison to previous concertos: There is no dialog between the solo piano and individual winds or groups of winds, as in the concertos, K. 453, 482 and 491. The chamber music element was held back here in favor of the soloist; the piano is no longer "Primus inter pares" but becomes virtually an autocratic protagonist. Several Mozart scholars (for example Marius Flothuis) see in this change of style a certain weakness, as if Mozart had lost interest in the form of the piano concerto, where all parts must be integrated. Such commentators overlook the fact that this work possesses an especially virtuosic piano part, which is at the same time easier played than that of the B-flat Concerto, K. 450, which, in Mozart's own words, "makes one sweat."

The reason for this exception—in view of the concerto's performances outside of Austria—is not difficult to recognize: Mozart conceived the Coronation Concerto as a "traveling concerto" that should be performable even where there was no first-class orchestra to be found or where no opportunity for rehearsal could be expected. He composed—fully intentionally!—the wind parts such that they could be omitted altogether! In Mozart's own written catalog of his works there is in particular this remark: Winds *ad libitum* (*"A Piano Concerto in D major – à 2 Violini, viola e basso / 1 flauto, 2 oboe, 2 fagotti, 2 corni, 2 clarini et Timpany ad libitum"*). Thus Mozart created a new, "Romantic" type of piano concerto that points far into the future. It is significant that exactly forty years later Chopin's piano concertos (at least that in F minor) were performed at private occasions first only with an accompanying string quintet (or quartet). The Coronation Concerto is, however, not a chamber concerto like K. 414 or 449, but rather a concerto for a virtuoso soloist, whose genre extends all the way to Rachmaninoff. Of course, a performance without winds would sound inadequate, especially in the tutti, and it was certainly conceived only as an emergency measure (and it would hardly be Mozart if despite all this, especially in the third movement, there were no captivating wind passages).

An ingenious harmonic subtlety in the first movement deserves further explanation: When the bass note G is added to the long note in the violins in the first tutti (m. 70), one inevitably hears a G minor harmony (B-flat rather than A-sharp). Only in the next measure does it in retrospect become clear that the A-sharp is a very long leading tone to B. In the parallel passage at the close of this movement (m. 395) there is however a "genuine" and passionate G minor!

Editor's suggestions are in gray. In a few cases where gray might be overlooked, we put such suggestions in brackets [ ], e.g. 3rd movement, mm. 43, 45.

Dynamics

It should be noted that Mozart wrote no dynamic indication for the solo part. Thus, all dynamic indications to be found in the piano part are the editor's suggestions and therefore in no way binding. Maybe they are too numerous; however, if played with discretion they might help the student to achieve a lively performance.

Staccato

Mozart used a variety of signs, ranging from clear strokes to dots. In this edition we have used mostly dots with which the modern performer is more familiar. In a few cases where confusion might arise, we used the wedge (drop), e.g. in the 3rd movement, mm. 42-45.

Continuo

Mozart's continuo indications have been reproduced in smaller print. It should be noted, however, that in Mozart's manuscript and in early prints, the continuo part was also notated in large type. It is well known that Mozart also used the solo pianoforte for continuo playing during the tutti in all his piano concertos. Normally it plays in unison with the violoncello and is silent when the lowest part is in the viola or in the bassoon. In modern performances this function is usually absent. However, if performed with a period instrument, whose sound mixes better with the orchestra than that of the modern piano, this practice is strongly recommended.

I believe that my new completion of the missing parts of this concerto comes closer to Mozart's intentions than the previously known versions, and it is my hope that this new version will lead to more frequent appearances of this impressive work on concert programs.

Paul Badura-Skoda, December 2004

List of Blank Spaces in Mozart's Autograph Score

First Movement

In the lower staff the following are missing:

mm. 81 – 107	mm. 292, 2ⁿᵈ quarter – 305
mm. 128 – 144	mm. 311, 2ⁿᵈ quarter – 328
mm. 161 – 171	mm. 340 – 342
mm. 174 – 176	mm. 344 – 352
mm. 236, 2ⁿᵈ quarter – 246, 1ˢᵗ quarter	mm. 381, 2ⁿᵈ quarter – 394
m. 250	mm. 401 – 404
mm. 263 – 277	

In the upper staff the following are missing:

m. 104, C# and D of the 3ʳᵈ and 4ᵗʰ beats	m. 132 ⎫ first slur
m. 152, G# of the first quarter	m. 356 ⎭

Second Movement

With the exception of the continuo in mm. 9 – 16, as well as mm. 35 (three last eighths) – 43, all notes of the lower staff are missing, as well as the notes in m. 105 of the upper staff.

Third Movement

In the lower staff the following are missing:

mm. 25 – 28, 1ˢᵗ eighth	mm. 213, 2ⁿᵈ eighth – 221
mm. 48 – 64	mm. 224 – 233
mm. 65, 2ⁿᵈ eighth – 66	mm. 238 – 255
mm. 67, 2ⁿᵈ eighth – 82	mm. 263, 2ⁿᵈ quarter – 265
mm. 87 – 104	mm. 269, 2ⁿᵈ quarter – 280
m. 108	mm. 284 – 286
mm. 113 – 114	mm. 288 – 295, 1ˢᵗ quarter
mm. 120 – 129	mm. 304 – 310
mm. 132 – 135	mm. 324, 2ⁿᵈ quarter – 348
mm. 147 – 151	mm. 350 – 354
mm. 173, 2ⁿᵈ eighth – 181	mm. 357 – 374
mm. 188 – 212	

In the upper staff the following are missing:

m. 28, 1ˢᵗ quarter	m. 7
m. 187	m. 59 ⎫
mm. 305 – 306 ⎫	mm. 97 – 98 ⎬ the gray slurs
m. 309 ⎬ the gray notes	m. 153 ⎭
mm. 336 – 338 ⎭	

Concerto
in D major

Edited and reconstructed by
Paul Badura-Skoda

W. A. Mozart, K 537
(1756-1791)

★ Andre:

* easier execution :

* m. 190, proposed execution:

* ms. 290: Two vertical strokes across this slur seem to indicate that Mozart cancelled it as an afterthought (autograph score).

* execution:

** mm. 330-332: These two measures are in fact in the rhythm of $\frac{3}{2}$, also earlier in mm. 146-148.

* Cadenza by P. Badura-Skoda, see p. 60

ad libitum

K 537

★ m. 42-45 : this wedge signifies an accent.

* André : one octave lower.

* m. 210, execution:

K 537

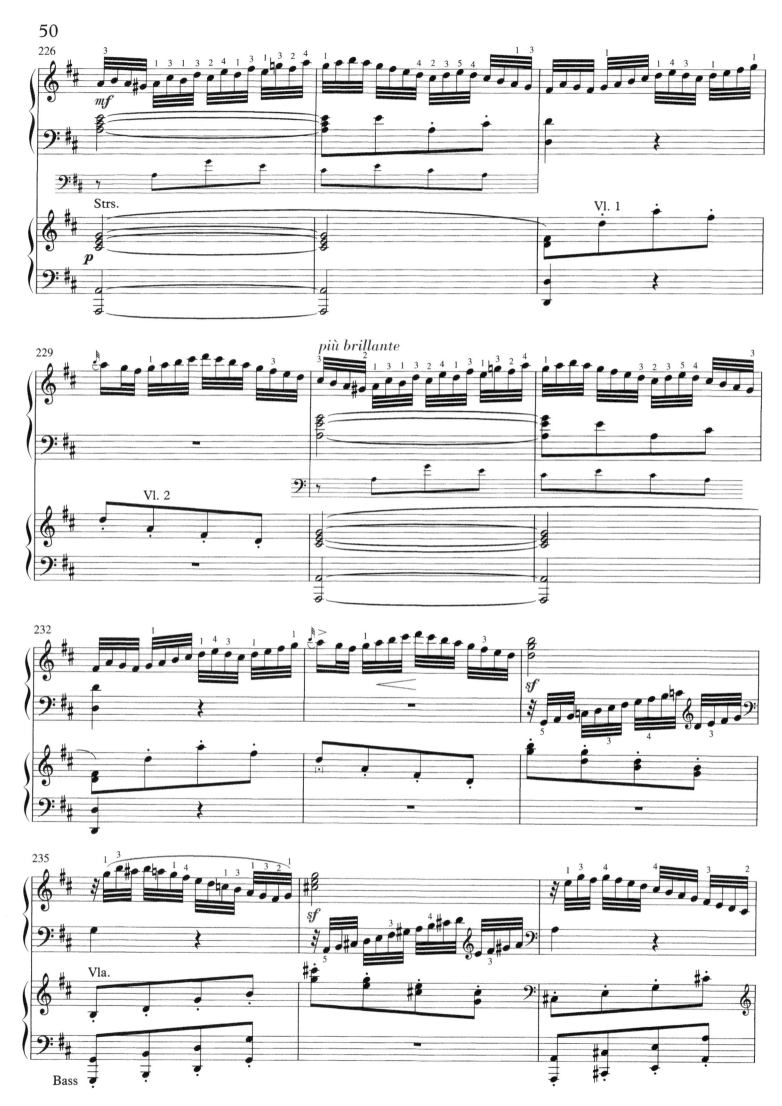

[Lead-in] *

299

303

307

311

* Lead-in by P. Badura-Skoda on page 63

gravure d. montel
logiciel «berlioz»

Cadenza – 1ˢᵗ movement, mes. 414

K 537

Lead-in – 2rd movement, mes. 70-71

Other Lead-in

Lead-in – 3rd movement, mes. 151

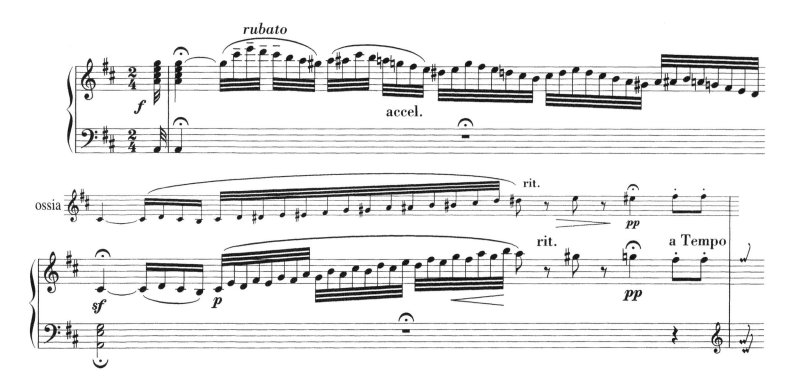

Lead-in – 3ʳᵈ movement, mes. 302

Inspired by Mozart's cadenza for the Variations K 573